Puppies

Children's Nature Library

GALLERY BOOKS
An Imprint of W. H. Smith Publishers Inc.

Louis Weber, C.E.O.
Publications International, Ltd.
7373 North Cicero Avenue
Lincolnwood, Illinois 60646

Printed in U.S.A.

8 7 6 5 4 3 2 1

ISBN 0-8317-6469-4

This edition published in 1991 by Gallery Books, an imprint of W.H. Smith Publishers, Inc., 112 Madison Avenue, New York, New York 10016.

Gallery Books are available for bulk purchase for sales and promotions and premium use. For details write or telephone the Manager of Special Sales, W.H. Smith Publishers, Inc., 112 Madison Avenue, New York, New York 10016; (212) 532-6600.

Written by Eileen Spinelli

Credits:
Animals/Animals: Norvia Behling: 5, 14, 16, 18, 19, 27, 29, 38, 55; Margot Conte: 46, 51; Jerry Cooke: 43; E.R. Degginger: 48; Ashod Francis: 52; Karen Tweedy Holmes: 9; Johnny Johnson: 32; Susan Jones: 20; Richard Kolar: 36; Zig Leszczynski: 4, 6, 10, 14, 52; Joe McDonald: 17, 63; Oxford Scientific Films/G.I. Bernard: 13, 36, 64; Robert Pearcy: Front Cover, 1, 3, 4, 6, 20, 22, 25, 30, 31, 34, 39, 41, 42, 44, 45, 48, 49, 53, 54, 56, 60, 62; John L. Pontier: 23; Michael & Barbara Reed: Back Cover; Ralph A. Reinhold: 11, 16, 46, 54, 57; Donald Specker: 7, 22, 24; Alfred B. Thomas: 30, 44, 50; J.R. Williams: 38; **Kent & Donna Dannen:** 32, 35; **FPG International:** Kenneth Garrett: 26; L. Grant: 28; Gary Randall: 61; **International Stock:** George Ancona: 8, 12; Mimi Cotter: 10; Bob Firth: 33, 40; Tom & Michele Grimm: 47; Michael Hendrikse: 37; Ronn Maratea: 15, 21; **Michael Schaeffler:** 26; **Tom Stack & Associates:** Barbara Von Hoffmann: 58, 59; **Unicorn Stock Photos:** John Ebeling: 36; Rod Furgason: 60.

Table of Contents

Introduction

Puppies are frisky bundles of fur. They are noisy and mischievous. They love to scamper, jump, and chase after things.

Like babies, puppies need care and attention. They need proper food. They also need to be kept clean, warm, and dry.

Introduction

How a puppy is treated is very important. If it is treated badly, it will grow up to cause problems. On the other hand, if a puppy is treated with gentle firmness and love, it will learn to like and trust people. Such a puppy will be obedient and healthy—it will bring its owners joy and delight.

There are over 400 different kinds of puppies. They come in all shapes, sizes, and colors. Each one is charming in its own way and so cute. Wouldn't you agree?

Mothers of Puppies

Mother dog chooses a safe, quiet place to give birth to her puppies. When they are born, she licks them clean. Then she cuddles them close so they can eat and stay warm.

A dog who has just had puppies is very protective of her babies. She does not want them to be disturbed. She may even snap at you if you get too close.

Mothers of Puppies

After her babies are born, mother dog stays with them. If a puppy cries, she comforts it. She teaches her puppies important lessons—like how to keep their bed nice and clean. She plays with them, too. If they get too rough or annoy her when she is taking a nap, she may scold them. Sometimes, she will even swat them with her paw if they do not behave.

Newborn Puppies

Newborn puppies cannot see or hear. Their eyes and ears are shut tight. They cannot walk either, but they can crawl. And crawl they do—right up to mother dog's soft, warm fur.

A puppy's first few days of life are spent sleeping and eating. If mother leaves the nest, puppy cries. When it becomes too tired to cry, it just cuddles close to its brothers and sisters.

Newborn Puppies

Newborn babies are tiny and frail and should not be handled for at least two weeks. By then, a puppy is stronger and quite adventurous. At three weeks old, it can see and hear. Oh, what a wonderful world…friendly faces, silly noises, and brand new toys!

A puppy should not be taken from its mother until it is about eight weeks old.

Puppy Talk

Puppies are noisy little creatures with high-pitched voices. Sometimes they bark when they are happy. Other times they bark when they are angry.

A growl means, "Don't bother me!" A yelp says, "Ouch! That hurts." If a puppy is left alone too long, it will whine. Sometimes when a puppy hears loud sirens or certain music, it will howl along.

Puppy Talk

A puppy talks with its tail, too. Tail wagging means, "I'm happy to see you!" A tail held low complains, "I'm nervous." A frightened

puppy will hold its tail between its legs.

Some puppies say "Hi" by sticking out their tongues. A puppy's ears also have plenty to say. Ears way back mean, "I'm scared." Ears erect ask, "What's going on?" When a puppy touches you with its paw, it wants to play.

Puppies & Play

Puppy's first toy is its mother. Playfully, it tugs at her ears and tail. Next, puppies discover that brothers and sisters can be fun. Often, two puppies will growl, chase, tumble, and nip. Don't worry. It's only a pretend fight. Most puppies love tug-of-war better than any other game. They also love to wrestle.

Puppies & Play

    A ball or a Frisbee will get a puppy to run and leap. Throw a stick, and a puppy will chase after it. It may even bring it back to you wagging its tail: "One more time, please!"

    Like all children, puppies love new toys. They often have a favorite. This is a toy that brings not only fun, but comfort, too.

Puppies & Baths

Young puppies should not be bathed at all. If your older puppy needs a bath, be sure the water is warm. Puppies don't like cold water.

Puppies hate getting soap in their eyes just like you do. But they do like to shake the bathwater from their coats. What splashes! Many puppies think baths are terrific. Other puppies, like many children, would rather play than bathe.

Puppies & Eating

All the food a newborn puppy needs is its mother's milk. As they grow older, puppies need solid food. They like meat, cereal, cheese, puppy chow, eggs, vegetables, and even baby food. Each puppy should have its very own dish. And never serve your puppy food that is too hot or too cold—room temperature is best.

Don't forget to always have a bowl of fresh water available for your puppy. An occasional biscuit or table scrap is alright, as long as you serve it in your puppy's dish. If you feed your puppy at the table, it will grow up to have bad manners. You should also never tease your puppy by eating treats in front of it unless you are willing to share.

Puppies & Sleep

The first night that a puppy must sleep without its mother, it will cry. A warm hot-water bottle tucked in its bed or a ticking clock wrapped in an old towel will be of comfort. Sometimes a softly playing radio or night-light will soothe a sleepy puppy. Many puppies even like to cuddle up with a cloth doll.

A store-bought bed is fine, but so is a cardboard box with a blanket. A puppy isn't fussy about how its bed looks as long as it is warm.

Unless you want a furry sleeping partner forever, never take a puppy into your bed. If you do, it will never want to sleep anywhere else.

Puppies Indoors

Puppies don't like to be left in the house all alone. If they are left for a long time, they will cry.

They are incredibly curious, too. They delight in exploring and getting into mischief. If a puppy smells cookies baking, it will scamper into the kitchen. "Sniff, sniff. What is that good smell?" If it hears the shower running, it will run up the stairs. "Scratch, scratch. What is that splashy noise?"

Puppies Outdoors

Like children, puppies need fresh air and sunshine. They love the exciting outdoors—they frolic in the cool grass, chase after bright butterflies, poke their noses into the garden, and nip at the wind.

Some hardy, thick-coated puppies may sleep outdoors when they get older. These puppies will need a doghouse that is sturdy and clean and keeps out the rain.

Puppies & Chewing

Puppies love to chew everything—shoes, slippers, leather schoolbags. They chew when they are bored or angry. They also chew just for fun. Puppies actually need to chew when they are teething.

If you don't want your puppy chewing your things, be sure it has its own things to chew. Nice crunchy dog biscuits, strong rawhide, large beef bones, and nylon bones are all good choices.

Puppies & Tricks

It is easy to teach a puppy tricks, as long as you don't confuse it with too many tricks at once.

Be sure to praise your puppy and reward it with a hug or a treat when it does well. If you are patient and gentle, you can easily teach your puppy to "beg," shake hands, chase balls, or knock at the door.

Puppies & Other Animals

Puppies get along well with other animals, especially if they are raised together. Puppies in training to be sheepdogs become loyal friends to the lambs in a flock. Kittens and puppies often enjoy each others' company. Farm puppies feel quite at home among the other farm animals.

Just remember that when you introduce your new puppy to another pet, give them both plenty of love and attention.

Yorkshire Terrier

The lively Yorkshire terrier (YAHRK-shir TER-ee-uhr) is also called a "Yorkie." These puppies were once trained to chase after rats in old factories and mines. Now they are popular as pets.

These puppies are clever little bundles of energy. They jump high, run after moving objects, and learn many things.

The short, fluffy coat of the Yorkie puppy will grow to be fine, silky, and long. This coat will need daily grooming.

Poodle

Don't be surprised to see a poodle performing in a circus, because these puppies are perky and smart. They love to entertain and "dance." Poodles are excellent swimmers, too.

They are also very glamorous. There are many different hairstyles for grown poodles—puppies only get trimmed. These puppies are very clean, and they don't shed. They can be as finicky as kittens when it comes to eating.

Cocker Spaniel

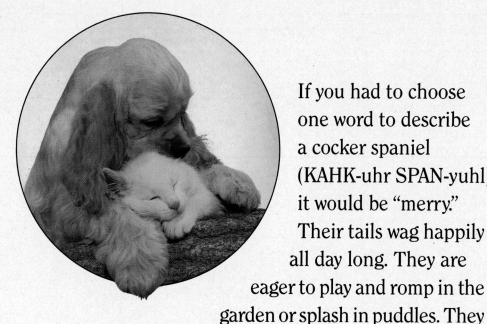

If you had to choose one word to describe a cocker spaniel (KAHK-uhr SPAN-yuhl), it would be "merry." Their tails wag happily all day long. They are eager to play and romp in the garden or splash in puddles. They delight in running and jumping. You will probably run out of energy long before your cocker spaniel gets tired. Cocker spaniel puppies are friendly to kittens and other puppies.

Collie

In Scotland, collie puppies were trained to look after sheep. They were even named after the "colley" sheep. The early settlers brought collies across the sea to America.

Collie puppies are frisky and full of fun. They seem to be born with a whimsical sense of humor. Even though these puppies take their time befriending strangers, once they do they are friends for life.

Beagle

Beagle puppies have long ears, big eyes, and sweet expressions. They are clean, smart, and easy to teach. They are also very, very curious. If a beagle puppy sniffs an interesting scent, it will go chasing after it. It isn't easy keeping up with a beagle. These puppies like plenty of space and lots of attention. Their coats are waterproof and their step is lively. Some beagle puppies are trained to hunt.

Golden Retriever

Golden retrievers (ri-TREE-vuhrz) are puppies that first came to us from Scotland. They are known for their pretty golden coats and gentle ways.

You can make a golden retriever happy by taking it for a romp in the park or teaching it to retrieve sticks and balls. These puppies also love children, kites, and water. They are very affectionate. They will nuzzle you until you pet them. These puppies will grow up to be strong, handsome, and fine hunters.

German Shepherd

Many German shepherd puppies grow up to be guide dogs for blind people. Puppies in training to be guide dogs wear special green coats to let people know who they are. They are taken to restaurants, shopping malls, buses, and trains. They even learn how to cross streets.

Other German Shepherd puppies are trained to be police dogs. Of course, many others grow up to be favorite pets.

Dalmatian

At birth, Dalmatian (dal-MAY-shuhn) puppies are pure white. Their spots appear gradually as they grow.

Dalmatian puppies are easy to train. They are cheery little creatures. If you are sad, they will perform silly tricks to make you smile. They are also clean and full of life.

Many Dalmatians grow up to be the beloved mascots of firehouses all over the world.

Saint Bernard

Saint Bernard puppies are cute and frisky, but they grow up to be big, powerful dogs.

These puppies often become the heroes of the dog world. They are very obedient and easy to teach. They are good at finding paths in deep snow. They like cold weather and aren't afraid in storms and blizzards. They have a great sense of where to go to rescue people in trouble.

Bloodhound

With their wrinkled skin and long, floppy ears, bloodhound puppies look rather homely. Actually, they are sweet, sensitive creatures with cheerful voices.

Of all puppies, the bloodhound has the best nose. It can follow even the faintest trail of scent. Many bloodhound puppies become detectives when they grow up. They help police officers find criminals and anxious parents find lost children. Bloodhounds are often trained not to bark.

Old English Sheepdog

Old English sheepdogs are often called "bobtails." They are fluffy little clowns that are always bouncing about. As they grow older, their coats become long and shaggy to protect them from the cold.

A bobtail in training to watch sheep will be raised with the lambs. This way, the lambs learn to trust the puppy as a friend. When this puppy grows up, it will bring in the sheep in a firm and gentle way.

Alaskan Malamute

As puppies, Alaskan malamutes (MAL-uh-MYOOTZ) are playful and adorable. When they grow up, however, they become quite dignified.

Alaskan malamutes have important work to do. They are trained to pull sleds across the ice and to haul heavy loads. They often race across the cold wilderness of the North. This rugged training begins when the puppy is about three months old.

Some people call the Alaskan malamute "King of the Working Dogs."